TRENDS IN SCANDINAVIAN TAXATION

Trends in Scandinavian Taxation

by

Gustaf Lindencrona

Professor, Jur. Dr.

Springer Science+Business Media, B.V. 1979

Cover design: Pieter J. van der Sman

Library of Congress Catalog Card Number: 79-16358

ISBN 978-90-200-0584-4 ISBN 978-94-017-4519-2 (eBook)
DOI 10.1007/978-94-017-4519-2

Originally published by Kluwer, Deventer, The Netherlands in 1979
Softcover reprint of the hardcover 1st edition 1979

Foreword

This book has been written as a preparatory work for the seminar on Scandinavian taxation of the XXXIII Congress of the International Fiscal Association in Copenhagen, 1979.

I wish to warmly thank professor Thøger Nielsen Copenhagen acting professor Olof Olsson, Helsingfors, and jur. dr. Fredrik Zimmer, Oslo, who have supplied the sections on the development of Danish, Finnish and Norwegian tax law, which have been included in the book. This valuable material, together with the corresponding Swedish information, has formed the basis for the analysis of trends, which appears in part II of the book.

I also want to extend my thanks to Peter Melz, Bachelor of economy, for help with the statistical material, to David Gerber, Attorney at law, New York, for translating parts of the book into English and to Ulla Lindqvist for typing the manuscript.

Stockholm, April 1979

Gustaf Lindencrona

Table of Contents

TABLE OF CONTENTS

Part I. Trends in Scandinavian Taxation 1965-1977

The overall tax level in Scandinavia is high compared to other industrialized countries. As shown in chart 1 this is the case for the whole period.

The size of the total tax revenue has increased rapidly over the period. Expressed in current prices the total tax revènue in 1977 is roughly 5-6 times larger than in 1965. Expressed in constant prices this means increases of 115% (Denmark), 122% (Finland), 138% (Norway), and 107% (Sweden) during the period.

With few exceptions the annual percentage increase in total tax revenue has exceeded the GDP[1]-growth. This has naturally resulted in an increased ratio when total tax revenue is compared to GDP (see Table 3). In 1965 the ratios were 30.3 (Denmark), 30.6 (Finland), 33.6 (Norway) and 35.6 (Sweden). In 1977 the ratios have increased to 45.0 (Denmark), 41.5 (Finland), 47.4 (Norway) and 53.4 (Sweden). Though the relationships between the countries are virtually the same in 1977 as they were in 1965, there were substantial variations in these relationships during the intervening period. As seen in chart 1 both Denmark and Norway had higher ratios than Sweden in the beginning of the 1970s.

The increase in the overall tax level is the result of increases in almost every important type of tax expressed as ratios of GDP. The size of increase differs, however, according to the type of tax. This is reflected in alterations in the composition of the total tax revenue.

The *taxes on income and profits (direct taxation)* in Scandinavia are on an international scale particulary significant revenue producers. Three out of the five OECD-countries (1977) where these taxes account for more than 20% of the GDP are Scandinavian. The fourth Scandinavian country (Norway) has a ratio that falls slightly below 20%.

Direct taxation as a percentage of total taxation has decreased significantly in Sweden. Norway shows a similar pattern although the decrease is less significant. In Denmark and Finland the trends are contrary to this.

Taxes of corporate income as a percentage of total tax revenue is decreasing in Finland (approximately from 8% to 4%) and Sweden (approximately from 5-6% to 3-4%). Expressed as a percentage of GDP the decrease is less significant. The decrease in the ratio of corporate tax to total tax revenue is therefore partly caused by the increases of other types of tax.

1. GDP = Gross Domestic Product at market prices.

In Denmark and Norway the corporate tax as a percentage of total tax revenue is normally 3-4% and although there are variations, no clear trend is seen. However, the tax base for the corporate tax (profits) is sensitive to variations in market conditions, which makes interpretations difficult.

Social security contributions is the type of tax that has the highest relative increase during the period in the Scandinavian countries, with the exception of Denmark. The increase varies from 2.5% in Finland (please observe that there are non-included social security contributions as mentioned in note 3), to 5.5% in Norway to 18% in Sweden.[2] In Denmark, on the contrary, the ratio has been reduced by one half from 2.2 to 0.9.

Despite the big increase it is only in Sweden that the social security contribution (1977) is the most important type of indirect tax (30.7%).

Taxes on consumption (general, as VAT, as well as specific taxes and customs on goods and services) were in the beginning of the period the dominant types of indirect taxes. With one exception, Sweden (where social security contributions as mentioned above have taken over this position), this position remains roughly the same over the period.

In Denmark there is a significant change in the composition of the consumption taxes. The specific consumption taxes have decreased from 31.5% to 19% expressed as ratios of total tax revenue. The general consumption tax has on the other hand increased from 9.1% to 19.5%. The decrease in consumption taxes in Sweden is assignable to the specific taxes (from 21.6% to 11.4% of total tax revenue). In Finland there is a decrease in specific consumption taxes, but in Norway no significant changes are seen.

A common trend in the Scandinavian countries (with the exception of Norway) therefore is the decrease in specific consumption taxes.

Taxes on net wealth and inheritance and gift taxes represent an insignificant ratio of the total tax revenue. In general the wealth tax is clearly more significant than the inheritance and gift tax. Together they rarely exceed 2% at any time in any country. With some reservations (substantial variations in different directions exist) this ratio is generally decreasing.

Taxes levied by local governments (no distinction as to different levels of local government is made) as a ratio of the total tax revenue (excluding social security contributions) roughly vary between 1/4 and 1/3 during the period. There are significant differences between countries for individual years, but the significance of these differences does not hold for the whole period. An increasing ratio can be seen in Denmark and Sweden, whereas no trend is significant in Finland and Norway.

The local taxes mainly consist of taxes on income and profit. Property taxes also play a certain role in Denmark and Norway.

---

2. Change in social security contributions as percentage of total tax revenue.

TRENDS IN SCANDINAVIAN TAXATION 1965 - 1977

CHART I

Total tax revenue as percentage of GDP

1965—1977

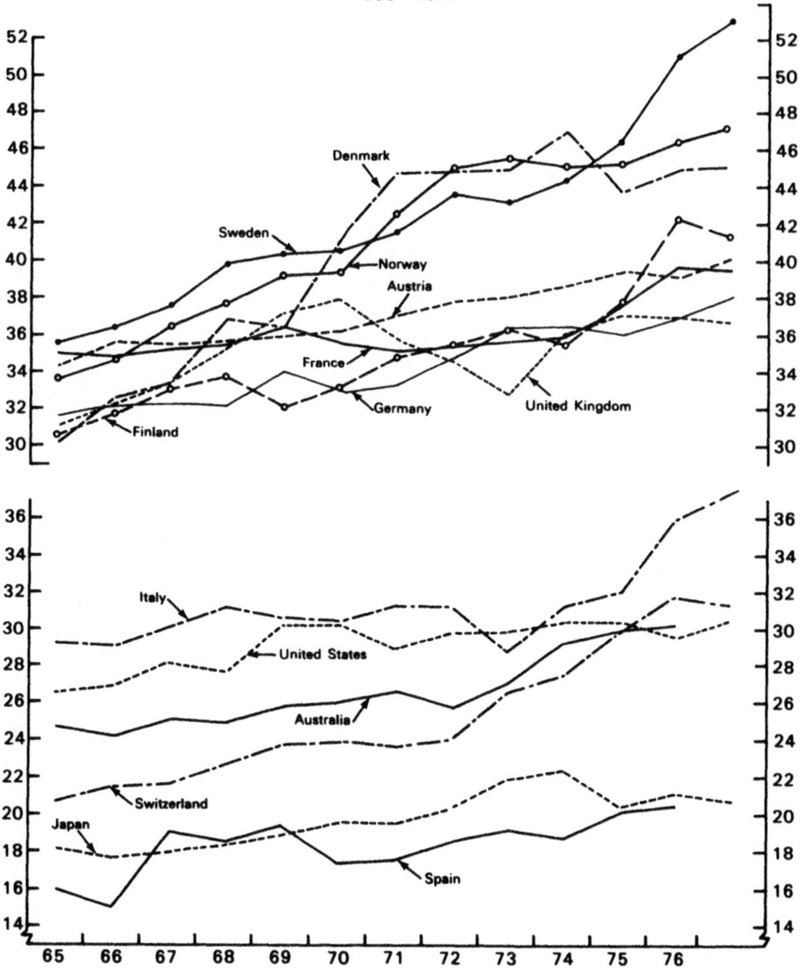

Source: OECD Revenue Statistics 1965-1977

TRENDS IN SCANDINAVIAN TAXATION 1965 - 1977

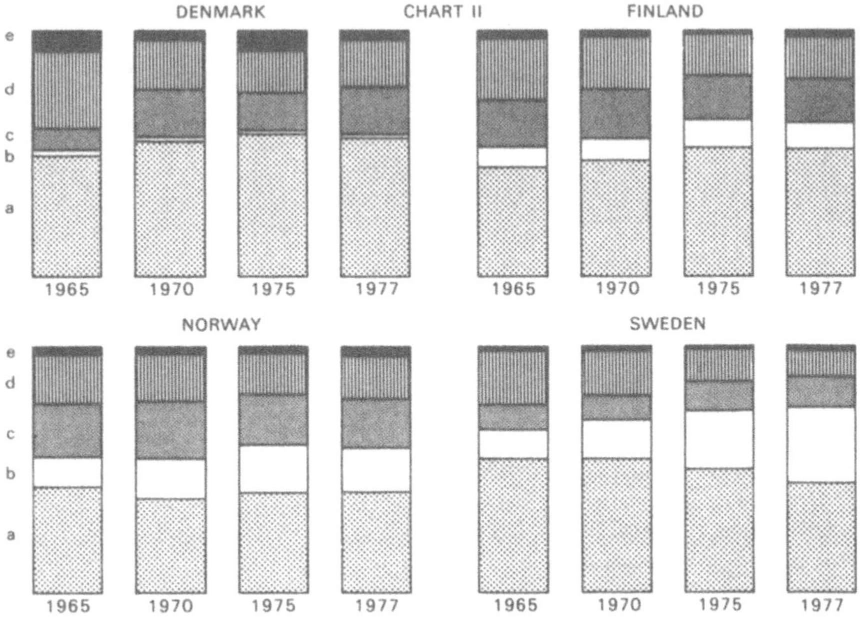

a) Taxes on income

b) Social security contributions

c) General taxes on consumption

d) Specific taxes on consumption

e) Residual post

TRENDS IN SCANDINAVIAN TAXATION 1965 - 1977

	Country	*National currency*	*Skr*	*US $*
1. Gross domestic product, billions of currency units, 1977*	Denmark	259.15	193.05	43.10
	Finland	119.85	133.27	29.75
	Norway	191.15	160.65	35.87
	Sweden	351.45	351.45	78.46
2. Total tax revenue in millions of currency units, 1977*	Denmark	116 700	86 936	19 409
	Finland	49 781	55 354	12 358
	Norway	90 675	76 208	17 014
	Sweden	187 617	187 617	41 887

* Preliminary figures.

	Country	1965	1966	1967	1968	1969	1970	1971	1972	1973	1974	1975	1976	1977*
3. Total tax revenue as percentage of GDP	Denmark	30,18	32,56	33,34	36,79	36,28	41,02	44,64	44,61	44,78	46,83	43,52	44,70	45,03
	Finland[3]	30,58	31,77	32,97	33,66	32,01	33,11	34,74	35,34	36,12	35,29	37,59	42,19	41,54
	Norway	33,59	34,59	36,47	37,66	39,12	39,26	42,40	44,86	45,32	44,88	45,01	46,18	47,44
	Sweden	35,64	36,44	37,58	39,81	40,31	40,45	41,49	43,50	43,02	44,18	46,32	50,89	53,38
4. Annual percentage change in GDP	Denmark	–	9,76	9,57	10,24	14,29	10,61	9,93	13,26	13,41	11,47	10,84	14,29	11,28
	Finland	–	7,55	8,39	13,42	14,23	11,74	9,34	15,21	21,56	26,10	16,38	11,01	10,21
	Norway	–	8,95	9,67	6,49	8,86	15,00	11,63	10,36	13,59	16,45	13,89	15,23	11,90
	Sweden	–	8,80	8,18	6,23	8,25	11,42	7,56	8,51	10,40	13,25	14,89	12,85	8,71
5. Annual percentage change in total tax revenue	Denmark	–	18,44	12,19	21,64	12,69	25,06	19,63	13,19	13,85	16,57	8,01	17,38	12,09
	Finland	–	11,75	12,49	15,78	8,64	15,57	14,71	17,19	24,24	23,23	23,97	24,60	8,69
	Norway	–	12,20	15,63	9,96	13,06	15,43	20,54	16,76	14,77	15,31	14,23	18,23	14,95
	Sweden	–	11,23	11,57	12,53	9,63	11,79	10,32	13,76	9,20	16,30	20,46	23,97	14,05
6. Total tax revenue (excl. social security) as percentage of GDP	Denmark	29,50	31,94	32,80	36,26	35,77	40,52	44,14	44,02	44,27	46,35	43,04	44,21	44,60
	Finland	28,07	29,22	30,01	30,69	29,14	30,14	31,43	32,01	32,43	31,73	33,54	37,51	37,04
	Norway	29,59	30,16	30,71	31,56	32,83	32,96	35,00	36,55	36,40	36,86	36,70	37,84	39,13
	Sweden	31,53	30,60	32,31	33,73	33,70	33,94	34,09	35,55	34,39	33,69	35,33	36,54	37,00

* Preliminary figures

3. Non-included social security contributions exist. As percentage of GDP they were 3%, 3.4%, 3.7% and 4%, 1974-1977.

DIFFERENT TAXES AS PERCENTAGE OF TOTAL TAX REVENUE

		1965	*1966*	*1967*	*1968*	*1969*	*1970*	*1971*	*1972*	*1973*	*1974*	*1975*	*1976*	*1977**
7. Denmark	a	44,62	45,84	46,53	46,04	45,79	51,41	54,90	54,39	54,58	58,23	54,81	54,09	52,61
	b	4,54	3,64	3,22	3,02	2,87	2,64	2,35	2,23	3,13	3,23	3,15	3,48	2,83
	c	2,23	1,91	1,65	1,45	1,38	1,22	1,12	1,31	1,14	1,03	1,11	1,09	0,94
	d	9,10	9,33	12,57	18,73	20,11	18,76	18,18	18,12	17,94	17,16	17,05	17,73	19,45
	e	31,50	31,14	27,90	23,89	23,64	19,95	17,69	18,21	17,05	14,46	17,86	17,94	19,02
	f	1,44	1,45	1,48	0,96	0,62	0,56	0,47	0,46	0,48	0,40	0,46	0,41	0,43
	g	0,65	0,56	0,54	0,50	0,44	0,35	0,29	0,38	0,37	0,34	0,38	0,40	0,34
8. Finland	a	35,89	37,23	38,14	38,61	41,10	41,88	42,62	43,60	44,63	46,92	48,18	49,26	47,49
	b	8,32	7,77	6,68	6,76	5,01	5,50	4,50	4,56	4,53	4,63	4,23	4,44	4,35
	c	8,21	8,04	9,00	8,83	8,98	8,99	9,53	9,42	10,21	10,09	10,77	11,08	10,84
	d	18,93	18,57	19,55	18,67	19,66	19,91	20,38	20,54	19,68	19,43	17,78	15,51	17,72
	e	24,59	19,20	20,40	24,55	22,89	21,45	20,88	19,75	18,68	16,62	16,98	16,59	17,30
	f	1,82	1,76	1,68	0,82	0,57	0,53	0,53	0,58	0,69	0,71	0,53	1,60	0,61
	g	0,22	0,27	0,26	0,25	0,28	0,25	0,23	0,21	0,21	0,25	0,23	0,23	0,27
9. Norway	a	39,61	39,39	38,38	39,51	38,76	35,17	34,34	35,59	36,24	37,87	37,88	36,61	36,58
	b	3,80	3,85	3,57	3,43	3,29	3,28	2,95	2,46	2,24	3,32	2,85	4,22	4,41
	c	11,93	12,79	15,79	16,21	16,08	16,05	17,46	18,51	19,68	17,86	18,46	18,06	17,52
	d	21,51	21,44	20,46	19,96	20,47	23,75	22,73	22,24	20,78	20,24	20,49	20,41	20,51
	e	19,36	18,97	17,86	17,38	17,77	18,55	19,43	17,84	17,45	16,19	16,76	17,37	17,74
	f	2,02	1,78	1,67	1,70	1,74	1,37	1,12	1,32	1,40	1,72	1,47	1,33	1,32
	g	0,27	0,21	0,19	0,21	0,21	0,24	0,21	0,21	0,22	0,26	0,22	0,16	0,12
10. Sweden	a	48,29	47,62	47,52	46,45	47,63	49,90	45,69	46,40	44,54	44,86	45,89	43,04	41,60
	b	6,08	5,01	4,60	4,96	4,87	4,42	3,65	3,97	4,31	3,42	4,32	3,57	2,82
	c	12,04	16,01	14,03	15,26	16,39	16,09	17,84	18,29	20,07	23,74	23,72	28,02	30,67
	d	10,27	12,14	12,35	12,17	11,02	10,29	14,25	14,30	14,36	12,93	11,91	12,37	12,59
	e	21,56	21,18	19,97	19,61	18,59	17,85	17,27	15,79	15,49	14,04	13,05	11,96	11,40
	f	0,90	0,76	0,74	0,77	0,72	0,71	0,60	0,56	0,54	0,39	0,49	0,40	0,39
	g	0,38	0,40	0,42	0,35	0,37	0,36	0,31	0,30	0,30	0,27	0,25	0,22	0,23

* Preliminary figures.

a. Individual taxes on income, profits and capital gains; b. Corporate taxes on profits and capital gains; c. Social security contributions and employers payroll or manpower taxes; d. General taxes on goods and services; e. Specific taxes on goods and services; f. Recurrent taxes on net wealth; g. Estate, inheritance and gift tax.

DIFFERENT TAXES AS PERCENTAGE OF GDP

		1965	*1966*	*1967*	*1968*	*1969*	*1970*	*1971*	*1972*	*1973*	*1974*	*1975*	*1976*	*1977**
11. Denmark	a	13,46	14,92	15,51	16,94	16,61	21,09	24,50	24,26	24,44	27,27	23,85	24,18	23,70
	b	1,37	1,19	1,07	1,11	1,04	1,08	1,05	0,99	1,40	1,51	1,37	1,56	1,27
	c	0,67	0,62	0,55	0,53	0,50	0,50	0,50	0,59	0,51	0,48	0,48	0,49	0,43
	d	2,75	3,04	4,19	6,89	7,29	7,70	8,12	8,08	8,03	8,04	7,42	7,93	8,76
	e	9,51	10,14	9,35	8,84	8,62	8,18	7,92	8,12	7,64	6,77	7,77	8,02	8,57
	f	0,43	0,47	0,50	0,35	0,23	0,23	0,21	0,20	0,21	0,19	0,20	0,18	0,19
	g	0,20	0,18	0,18	0,18	0,16	0,15	0,13	0,17	0,17	0,16	0,16	0,18	0,15
12. Finland	a	10,97	11,83	12,58	13,00	13,16	13,87	14,80	15,40	16,12	16,56	18,11	20,78	19,72
	b	2,54	2,47	2,20	2,28	1,61	1,82	1,56	1,61	1,64	1,63	1,59	1,87	1,81
	c	2,51	2,55	2,97	2,97	2,87	2,98	3,31	3,33	3,69	3,56	4,05	4,68	4,50
	d	5,79	5,90	6,45	6,29	6,29	6,59	7,08	7,26	7,11	6,86	6,68	6,54	7,36
	e	7,52	6,10	6,72	8,26	7,33	7,10	7,25	6,98	6,75	5,87	6,38	7,00	7,18
	f	0,56	0,56	0,56	0,27	0,18	0,18	0,18	0,20	0,25	0,25	0,20	0,68	0,25
	g	0,07	0,08	0,09	0,09	0,09	0,08	0,08	0,07	0,08	0,09	0,09	0,10	0,11
13. Norway	a	13,31	13,63	14,18	14,88	15,16	13,81	14,56	15,96	16,43	17,00	17,05	16,91	17,35
	b	1,28	1,33	1,30	1,29	1,29	1,29	1,25	1,10	1,01	1,49	1,28	1,95	2,09
	c	4,01	4,42	5,76	6,11	6,29	6,30	7,40	8,30	8,92	8,01	8,31	8,34	8,31
	d	7,22	7,41	7,46	7,52	8,01	9,33	9,64	9,98	9,42	9,09	9,22	9,43	9,73
	e	6,50	6,56	6,51	6,55	6,95	7,28	8,24	8,00	7,91	7,26	7,54	8,02	8,42
	f	0,68	0,62	0,61	0,64	0,68	0,54	0,48	0,59	0,63	0,77	0,66	0,62	0,63
	g	0,09	0,07	0,07	0,08	0,08	0,09	0,09	0,10	0,10	0,12	0,10	0,07	0,06
14. Sweden	a	17,21	17,35	17,86	18,49	19,20	20,18	18,96	20,18	19,16	19,82	21,26	21,90	22,20
	b	2,17	1,82	1,73	1,97	1,96	1,79	1,51	1,73	1,85	1,51	2,00	1,81	1,51
	c	4,29	5,84	5,27	6,08	6,61	6,51	7,40	7,95	8,63	10,49	10,99	14,26	16,38
	d	3,66	4,42	4,64	4,84	4,44	4,16	5,91	6,22	6,18	5,71	5,52	6,29	6,72
	e	7,68	7,72	7,51	7,81	7,49	7,22	7,16	6,87	6,67	6,20	6,04	6,09	6,07
	f	0,32	0,28	0,28	0,31	0,29	0,29	0,25	0,25	0,23	0,17	0,23	0,21	0,21
	g	0,14	0,15	0,16	0,14	0,15	0,15	0,13	0,13	0,13	0,12	0,12	0,11	0,12

* Preliminary figures.

a. Individual taxes on income, profits and capital gains; b. Corporate taxes on profits and capital gains; c. Social security contributions and employers payroll or manpower taxes; d. General taxes on goods and services; e. Specific taxes on goods and services; f. Recurrent taxes on net wealth; g. Estate, inheritance and gift tax.

	1965	*1966*	*1967*	*1968*	*1969*	*1970*	*1971*	*1972*	*1973*	*1974*	*1975*	*1976*	*1977*
15. DENMARK													
Local Government tax revenue*	–	5 087	6 079	6 920	8 096	11 014	14 304	16 263	20 707	23 088	26 487	31 036	
Local Government tax revenue as percentage of total tax revenue (excl. social security)		23	25	21	21	23	25	25	28	27	30	30	
Central Government tax revenue as percentage of total tax revenue (excl. social security)		77	75	79	79	77	75	75	72	73	70	70	
FINLAND													
Local Government tax revenue*	1 892	2 140	2 366	2 645	2 964	3 474	3 926	4 460	5 489	6 951	9 217	11 015	
Local Government tax revenue as percentage of total tax revenue (excl. social security)	26	27	27	25	26	26	26	25	25	26	28	27	
Central Government tax revenue as percentage of total tax revenue (excl. social security)	74	73	73	75	74	74	74	75	75	74	72	73	

* In national currency units.

	1965	*1966*	*1967*	*1968*	*1969*	*1970*	*1971*	*1972*	*1973*	*1974*	*1975*	*1976*	*1977*
NORWAY													
Local Government tax revenue*	4 366	4 911	5 408	5 953	6 609	7 493	8 637	9 632	11 302	13 004	15 116	18 882	
Local Government tax revenue as percentage of total tax revenue (excl. social security)	29	33	33	30	29	28	28	27	28	27	28	29	
Central Government tax revenue as percentage of total tax revenue (excl. social security)	71	67	67	70	71	72	72	73	72	73	72	71	
SWEDEN													
Local Government tax revenue*	8 838	11 037	13 060	14 566	15 941	17 344	20 052	24 515	26 912	29 372	33 935	40 055	
Local Government tax revenue as percentage of total tax revenue (excl. social security)	25	29	30	30	31	30	32	35	36	35	34	34	
Central Government tax revenue as percentage of total tax revenue (excl. social security)	75	71	70	70	69	70	68	65	64	65	66	66	

* In national currency units.

Explanations

Tables 1 - 14

Source: OECD Revenue Statistics 1965-76, with the following exceptions.
Tables 7-14 (part e-g), 10 c and 14 c, concerning the years 1966 and 1967, are based on OECD Revenue Statistics 1965-74. There appears to be minor discrepancies between the two editions.

Table 15

Source: Data for local government tax revenue has been derived from the Statistical Abstracts for the different countries.
Data for total tax revenue is based on the above mentioned OECD material. Central government tax revenue has been calculated by subtracting local government tax revenue from total tax revenue (excl. social security). The reservation made above for 1966 and 1967 is valid for the OECD material in this table too.

Part II. Special Features of the Scandinavian Development

1. The Common Scandinavian Background

The links between the Scandinavian countries are strong. These links are not, however, predominantly of a legal nature even if a number of treaties exist between the Scandinavian states. Much more important is the common cultural background, the similarities in social and political conditions and the more or less common history. Language is of course an important factor. The Swedish Danish, and Norwegian languages are so close to each other that they are easily understood in all Scandinavia. Finnish is of course very different but there is a Swedish speaking minority in Finland and an important part of the Finnish-speaking population in Finland masters the Swedish language.

In the legal field there is a long tradition of co-operation. Important laws, especially civil laws, are worked out by joint Scandinavian efforts. The new corporation law is a recent example.

In the tax field such co-operation does not exist to the same extent. It is nonetheless strong. Contacts between the ministries are regular as they are between the universities. The Nordic Scientific Council for Tax Research is an important example of Scandinavian co-operation. It should not be forgotten that even if new legislation in the tax field is not the result of a common Scandinavian effort, the Scandinavian legislators borrow freely from each other. A succesful tax innovation in one Scandinavian country will soon be copied in the other countries.

In the first part of this book the trends in Scandinavian taxation were described with the help of statistics. In this part questions of a more specific legal nature will be treated. They have not been chosen to answer the more general question of whether there is a tendency towards convergence of the Scandinavian tax systems or not. They have been chosen because they show typical features in the recent development of income taxation and, particularily, how common trends in Scandinavian taxation are the result of common social, economic or ideological pressures on the tax system.

2. Extension of the Tax Base

Income taxation was originally founded very much on the same principles in the Scandinavian countries. According to the 'source' theory, tax laws enumerated certain sources of income, and the concept of income was defined to be the revenue flowing from these sources. Capital gains were thus not included in the concept of income. They were only taxed when they were regarded as 'speculative', i.e. the result of a certain mental effort. Generally a capital gain was supposed to be speculative if the asset had been acquired by a commercial transaction and not held for more than a certain period of time.

In all Scandinavian countries, however, business income was calculated according to a wider concept of income. Sound accounting practices were to a large extent accepted as governing the concept of business income.

In Sweden farm income has recently been deemed to resemble business income and almost identical rules have been adopted. The other Scandinavian countries have not gone that far in this respect.

The recent dominant trend in all Scandinavian countries regarding the tax base has been the gradual inclusion of capital gains in the tax base. The lines of development have, however, been different. Finland has, for example, not gone as far as the other countries. Different methods have also been employed. In Denmark capital gains are taxed as 'special income' at a flat rate of now 50%. In Sweden capital gains are supposed to form a category of income of their own, and a capital gain in thus added to other income of the taxpayer. The tax on the capital gain will therefore depend on the other income of the taxpayer. In Norway both methods have been used.

There are similarities in the technical details, too. It might be noted that in Denmark, Norway, and Sweden capital gains on real property generally are adjusted for inflation.

It could not been said that the gradual widening of the tax base and especially the inclusion of capital gains in the tax base is an answer to fiscal needs. The revenue produced hardly makes the administrative efforts worth while. This is especially true for the taxation of shares. The development must instead be seen as a result of a changing concept of justice in the tax field calling for more equality in the tax treatment of different types of income.

Denmark

In accordance with the classical income definition the Danish income tax code expressly states that capital gains or capital losses shall not be taken into consideration when computing taxable income. Only few exceptions were made notably in respect of payment for the sale of goodwill until a separate tax code dealing with the taxation of 'special income' was introduced in the late fifties. Under the label 'special income' which should be taxed at a flat rate of 30% a great number of receipts of different nature were dealt with in the same code. Among the cases covered by this extended tax base were gains obtained on several types of capital assets especially shares and real property. The relationship between ordinary income and special income is obvious although special income is taxed separately if obtained by physical persons. However, a negative special income can be deducted from ordinary income and vice versa a negative ordinary income reduces a positive special income. It is therefore natural to regard the special income as an extension of the general tax base. This has become even more apparent after successive increases of the special income tax which now amounts to 50%. The special income tax has caused many difficulties. First it should be mentioned that it was felt necessary in respect of real property to introduce deductions when computing gain in order to reflect the inflationary development of prices in respect of real estate. Such deductions have till now not been accepted in respect of goodwill or shares and the legislation thus suffers under a lack of neutrality. Furthermore there are many examples of capital gains not covered by the code. For instance, the gain from sale of personal property and valuables and perhaps most important: gain from the sale of private homes. The special income concept has never been a fiscal success and its lack of consistency and the fact that it generally disregards the inflation as the background of what is called taxable gain has made this legislation an object of criticism and political struggle. It has also been a factor complicating the transfer of a family business on death. The last mentioned problem led to special legislation with the aim of facilitating the transfer of agricultural property by gift which is ordinarily treated as a sale.

In respect of private homes the present government has proposed a tax based on the increase of value – a proposal which may change the present structure of 'special income'.

It should, however, also be mentioned that a total restructuring of the taxation of shares has been proposed and that this may lead to a reduction of the tax burden on the sale of shares.

In another area – the taxfree foundations – a government commission is working investigating the possibility of extending the tax base.

Private foundations with several characteristics in common with a fully discretionary trust are only subject to a limited tax liability and have therefore in many cases been used as holders of shares in family corporations. A gain on the sale of the shares realized by the foundation is not taxable.

The hottest issue in Danish income taxation has been the question whether the deductibility of interests can and should be limited to commercial debts, excluding private interests. Till now no definite answer has been given, neither politically, nor technically. (See 5. Taxation of owner-occupied dwellings.)

Finland[1]

Depending on whether the income derives from business activity, agriculture or other sources, one can with respect to the tax base distinguish between three main types of income, namely business income, farm and forestry income and personal income. The three laws in which the tax bases for these types of income are defined utilize income concepts which in part differ from each other.

The rules which establish the tax base for the taxation of personal income continue to be based to a large extent on the same restrictive income concept which was used in the legislation in which income taxation in its modern form was introduced to Finland in the 1920's. Thus capital gains are there still non-taxable to a large extent. According to the main rule capital gains on personal assets are entirely exempted if the seller has aquired the asset as a gift, inheritance or bequest or has owned it for at least 10 years in the case of real property, and for at least 5 years in the case of shares or other movables. In the case of real property a gradually mitigated taxation is applied after 6 years of ownership. Capital gains from the sale of the taxpayers' residence are, regardless of these time limits, exempted if he has owned the place and used it as his or his family's permanent residence for at least one year immediately prior to the sale, and if he buys himself a new residence within a certain time. In those cases where capital gains are taxable, their 'face amount' (that is, the full amount, without correction for inflation) is taxed as ordinary income. Capital losses are deductible only by way of exception.

The narrowness of the income concept is also indicated by the fact that most *social* and other *income* transfers from the public sector to the household sector – such as National old age and disability pensions, sickness and unemployment allowances and housing subsidies – are exempted from tax and that *imputed income* is taxable only in limited cases. It can be noted in addition that as a kind of carry-over from the economically difficult years after World War II which has now become more or less integrated into the tax system *interest* on ordinary bank deposits as well as on most bonds is exempted when received by individuals.

Regarding deductibility of outlays, it may finally be mentioned that only interest on credits related to business or farming is deductible without significant limitations. Interest on housing loans and mortgages for instance is deductible only up to 15 000 mks (about 4000 US dollars) a year and interest on consumption credits only up to 5000 mks (about 1250 US dollars) a year.

The provisions according to which taxable *business income* is determined are

1. For further information regarding the Finnish tax system, see the following articles by Lasse Aarnio: 'Development in Finnish taxation 1965-1976', 'Direct taxation in Finland' and 'Indirect taxation and social security contributions in Finland' in the Bank of Finland Monthly Bulletins of, respectively, January 1978 (pp. 20-27), July 1978 (pp. 20-29) and September 1978 (pp. 20-25).

based on modern accounting principles. The tax base is in this case rather broad; in principle all business receipts are taxable income while all business outlays and losses, except income tax and other direct taxes, are deductible. There is, however, one important exception to this main rule: Capital gains derived from transfer of real property held for at least 10 years as well as securities held for at least 5 years are, when the assets belonged to the fixed assets of the business, exempted from tax. The close connection between the tax provisions and the accounting principles is also obvious in that most of the hidden reserves that the taxpayer is allowed to create in his financial statement, by undervaluation of inventories, rapid depreciations of fixed assets and reservations for future outlays, are accepted also in tax legislation.

Farm income, except forestry income, is determined according to principles similar to those just mentioned. Capital gains derived from transfers of farm land and forest land are not regarded as farm income, but as personal income, and are thus asually tax free. In contrast to the previously mentioned types of income *forestry income* is not taxed on an actual income basis but on a presumptive basis in accordance with a special method of area or acreage taxation. According to this method, the owner of forest land is taxed on the forest's presumed growth.

The *tax on net wealth* can be regarded, to a certain extent, as an extra income tax on capital income. In the wealth taxation the tax base is, in principle, the taxpayer's total net wealth. There are, however, quite a few exceptions both to the rule that all the taxpayer's assets should be taken into account and to the rule that the assets should be taken into account at current values. These exceptions are not always very well co-ordinated with the way in which the corresponding income is treated in the taxation of income.

At present there are no definite plans for major changes with respect to the tax base. Within the not too distant future one should, however, expect taxation of gains on the sale of personal assets to be subjected to taxation. When this happens, the prerequisities will have been established for reducing the severity of the wealth tax and improving co-ordination of the rules for income and wealth taxation.

Norway

Extension of the tax base in recent years has mainly occurred in the area of capital gains taxation. The original starting point – back in the previous century – was that such gains did not constitute taxable income. The capital gains of a business have, however, long been considered taxable. Moreover, for capital gains other than those of a business the main rule has long been that such gains are taxable if the property has been disposed of within ten years after acquisition or was acquired for the purpose of speculation. Gains on the sale of parcels of land were always taxable, and gains on the sale of stock outside of a business were always nontaxable, where not more than approximately 30% of the capital of the company is sold. Gains on the sale of furniture and other household goods were nontaxable.

Nonbusiness capital gains taxation has been extended three times in recent years. In 1971 gains on transfers of usage rights in real property and gains on the sale of depreciable business property were made taxable regardless of how long they had been held prior to transfer. Later the same year a special law was passed concerning the taxation of capital gains on the sale of stock. Such capital gains – which had previously been nontaxable – are, according to the new law, to be taxed at a rate of 50% if the sale is made within five years after the end of the acquisition year. Losses on similar transactions are deductible against capital gains on the sale of stock, which are taxable according to this law, but not against other income.

In 1974 the rules on capital gains taxation were substantially revised. According to this revision, the basic principle is now that all capital gains – including nonbusiness capital gains – are taxable. Special exceptions were, however, included with the result that the effects of the changes are not overly significant. The special law of 1971 continues to be applicable with respect to nonbusiness capital gains on the sale of stock, and gains on personal property such as furniture remain nontaxable. Gains on the sale of active farms – including forestry – as well as on the sale of one's personal residence are taxable only when the sale takes place within ten years after acquisition.

The most important change in 1974 was thus that gains on the sale of rented residential properties became taxable, regardless of the lenght of the holding period. This was also the main goal of the revision. Norwegian law continues to have a provision that certain properties acquired by inheritance may be sold without tax. This provision is, however, generally considered to be an anachronism and is expected to be eliminated in the near future.

It should also be mentioned that taxation may be deferred in many instances for an indefinite period if an amount corresponding to the amount received is reinvested in another object of the same type. This applies, for example, to business assets and, in certain cases, to farms (including forestry), but it does not apply to stocks or to goodwill. In 1966 such defferral was also made possible for gains on the sale of one's personal residence.

With regard to the calculation of gains it should be noted that rules have been introduced in recent years providing for a certain amount of inflation adjustment on the base value of real property. There are, however, no corresponding provisions for other types of property.

As to property which has been inherited there have been proposals to the effect that the heir should take over his benefactor's basis in such property rather than applying the current market value at the time of death, as is presently provided. This proposal has not, however, been the subject of serious consideration by the parliament.

In certain other areas there have been examples of restrictions of the tax base.

For example, a 1977 revision of the law provided that certain types of payments in kind would no longer be taxable, provided certain conditions were met.

Sweden

The tax base is in Sweden somewhat different for different categories of income. The concept of *business income* is rather wide. It includes whatever flows into the business in the form of money, goods and other benefits, provided that the receipt is one that may normally be expected to arise in the course of a business operation. Gains from the sale of capital assets are generally included, the reason probably being the generous rules of depreciation of these assets. It makes no difference if the enterprise is incorporated or not. Some gains are not, however, included in business income, for example gains on shares and real estate. They are taxed according to the capital gains rules. *Farm income* is regarded as a special category of income. The rules are, however, since 1972 mainly the same as for business income. The 1972 reform increased the tax base of farm income substantially. The reason was the increasingly business-like character of modern farming.

For other categories of income, that is, *housing income, personal income* and *capital income* a more limited tax base is still used. In practice, however, the tax base has been enlarged substantially for all taxpayers in Sweden, engaged in business or not. This has been done by important changes in the rules of the taxation of *capital gains*. Capital gains are not taxed separately in Sweden. They form, however, a category of income of its own with its own rules for the determination of income.

In 1966 special rules were introduced for shares and in 1967 special rules were enacted for the taxation of capital gains on real property. The specific rules have since been changed, but the general principles introduced in 1966 and 1967 remain in effect.

The 1966-1967 reforms meant a considerable enlargement of the tax base. Previously all capital gains had been tax-free after a certain time (10 years for real property, 5 years for movable property). If the seller had acquired the asset by gift, inheritance or bequest the capital gain was tax-free.

Today, however, a capital gain on real property or shares is taxed regardless of how the asset was acquired. If it is acquired by gift, inheritance or bequest both the length of the holding period and the amount of gain must be determined by going back to the last preceding commercial acquisition. When real property is sold the whole gain must be included in taxable income regardless of how many years it has been owned by the seller. On the other hand the cost of the property may be multiplied by a coefficient or index number to take account of the changes in the price level. If the sale gives rise to a taxable capital gain the payment of the tax can be postponed, provided the seller lived in the sold house and acquires a new house to live in. Taxation of gains arising from inflations is thus avoided in this case. This is not the case for shares. On the other hand, only

40% of the gain is included in taxable income.

3. Intregration of Corporation Tax and Income Tax

Economic double taxation is on its way to disappear in all the Scandinavian countries. The same methods have not been chosen, however, to accomplish an integration of the tax on the corporation and the tax on the share-holders.

Norway has evidently gone furthest and abolished double taxation of income completely for dividends made of current profits. (It exists, however, for the net wealth tax). The differences existing between local taxation and national taxation in this regard are of a technical character, not a conceptual one. For local tax purposes it has been necessary to keep the taxation of the corporation to give the 'source' municipality the right to tax. Finland has moved in the same direction but not as far.

In Denmark integration is realized only to a minor extent. The difference between the method used in Denmark and the other Scandinavian countries is of course explained by Denmark's membership in the European Community. Denmark is the only Scandinavian country that has up to now chosen the imputation system.

The Swedish system is different from the others in several respects. The deduction allowed to the corporation is only given up to a certain maximum percentage of the paid-in capital, it is limited in time and it is permitted only for newly issued shares. The Swedish system could therefore in some respects more properly be regarded as a stimulus for corporation expansion than as a measure for avoiding double taxation.

There is certainly a common trend in the Scandinavian tax systems that double taxation is disappearing. There is, however, uncertainty about the methods. The Scandinavian countries have chosen different approaches. No country seems, however, to be satisfied with its own method and the disadvantages are widely discussed. The present situation in this field could be said to be one of uncertainty.

Denmark

In 1977 the integration of company tax and personal income tax was accepted in principle. It was however, only carried through in a very modified way. The shareholders get a compensation corresponding to 15 % of dividends – which in reality means that about 25 % of corporate tax is refunded. The technical complications of the system (including a special 'précompte' – 'udligningsskat' in the companies) have been so great that it is doubtful if this legislation will get a long life.

Finland

With regard to local taxation, the rules concerning taxation of stock companies and their shareholders are based on the classical system. Thus there is no integration of the income taxation of the corporation and that of its shareholders.

This was also true to a large extent with regard to national income taxation until 1969, when a split-rate system was introduced. Under the current system corporations are entitled to deduct 60 % of paid-out dividends (minus any received dividends) against their taxable income. To the extent dividends related to newly-issued stock (i.e. stock which is less than 6 years old) they are generally deductible up to 100 %. On the stockholders' side the remaining double taxation is reduced by a special dividend income deduction which has the effect that for individuals the dividends of domestic corporations are non-taxable insofar as they do not exceed 1500 mks (about 400 US dollars).

Chain or 'snowball' taxation of the income of corporations is precluded according to the main rule on both the local and national levels. Thus dividends paid by one Finnish corporation to another will not be considered taxable income unless the receiving corporation is a dealer in securities or a holding company with limited redistribution (less than 80 %) of dividends received.

Adoption of an imputation system has been discussed but does not – at least at the moment – appear likely.

Norway

The rules concerning taxation of that portion of corporation profits which are distributed to its shareholders in the form of dividends differ, depending on whether local or national taxation is involved. According to the principles of local taxation, the rule has long been that the corporation is fully taxed, without any deduction for distributed dividends. In return the dividends cannot be taxed to the shareholder. With regard to national tax rules there previously was a system of double taxation, but a 1963 law made possible deductions on the corporate level for dividends on newly-issued stock. And in 1969 this deduction was expanded to include old shares, provided the dividends did not exceed the corporation's profits for the year. If the shareholder is domiciled outside of Norway, a 25 % withholding tax is applicable, although tax treaties often provide a lower rate.

The issue of revising these rules has recently been discussed, especially with regard to the fact that Norway has relatively limited taxation rights when a stockholder is domiciled outside the country, but an official proposal to this effect has not yet been made. It may be noted that in the area of wealth taxation double taxation at the national level was reintroduced in 1972.

Sweden

In 1960 the so-called Annell law was enacted on a provisional basis. According to this law corporations were given the right to deduct the amount of dividends paid out on new shares issued for cash or property between January 1, 1961 and December 31, 1970. The deduction was limited to 4 % per year of the amount paid in for the shares and could be used for six years.

In 1967 the law was prolonged. For shares paid for after June 30, 1966 corporations can deduct 5 % of the amount paid in for the shares during a maximum period of ten years. Recently the law has been changed again. For shares paid for after December 31, 1978 the maximum annual deduction is now 10 %. The government does not think that time has come yet for the introduction of an imputation system on the EC model in Sweden.

According to the present rules deductions cannot exceed 100 % of the amount paid for the shares. The deduction must be taken not later than 20 years later than the date of the payment for the shares. Because of the intercorporate dividend exemption the deduction for new shares cannot be made if more than half of the shares are owned by another Swedish corporation. This rule is rather clumsy and one of the shortcomings of the legislation.

The right to deduct dividends on new shares is extended to corporations paying dividends to foreign shareholders as long as withholding tax is paid to Sweden. This means that in some cases foreign-owned subsidiaries are in a better position than Swedish-owned ones.

These rules could be regarded as a partial integration of the tax on corporation and individual income. The main feature of the legislation is that the right of deduction is not extended to older shares. This is a part of an effort of the Swedish tax legislator to stimulate expanding corporations without giving benefits to more stagnant corporations and their shareholders.

4. The Progress of Separate Taxation

Social and economic conditions in the Scandinavian countries are very similar. The same could be said for public debates. The same topics are generally discussed at the same time in the Scandinavian countries.

Originally there was not much debate about joint taxation. This principle was supposed to be more or less self-evident. Marriages were stable, the husband was the only bread-winner and the ability to pay taxes was consequently measured by the income of the household instead of the income of each individual.

When joint taxation is abolished it is because of both new economic conditions and new ideas. It has been widely discussed in the Scandinavian countries if, and in that case to what extent, the willingness to work and make extra efforts is influenced by taxation. Opinions have been very different. As to joint taxation and the willingness of women to work outside the household the effect was, however, obvious to everyone. In a country with strongly progressive income tax rates the net effect of a woman's employment was very small if her husband was already gainfully employed. At a time when the demand for labour was very high it seemed evident that it would increase the labour force substantially if separate taxation was introduced. This argument, however, seemed to be valid only for earned income. To interest women in working it seemed necessary to introduce a system of separate taxation for earned income only.

The ideological aspects should not, however, be completely overlooked. The older ideas about joint taxation were firmly entrenched. In several Scandinavian countries official committees recommended joint taxation in spite of the fact that the economic situation was changing rapidly. The efforts of womens' organisations and other organisations and individuals interested in the progress of sexual equality were needed to accomplish the changes. Their ideological arguments favoured the complete abolishment of joint taxation. Each individual was to be regarded as an independent unit.

The result in all the Scandinavian countries has been a sudden breakthrough of separate taxation. Different stages in this development can, however, be distinguished. The first step is generally the introduction of measures providing for the possibility of separate taxation of earned income at the request of the taxpayer. The next step is generally the introduction of mandatory separate taxation of earned income. As farm income and business income present special problems they are generally put aside when separate taxation is introduced. The maintenance of joint taxation only for special groups for formal reasons (e.g. where only one of the spouses is regarded as proprietor of the farm or business) is resented by the groups left out. After some years the pressure from these groups results in the introduction of some kind of separate taxation for them also. Different technical solutions are found in different Scandinavian countries.

The last step, the introduction of complete separate taxation, has not been taken in any Scandinavian country. Unearned income and net wealth is still taxed jointly. The reason for this is to a large extent another important factor in Scandinavian taxation: the growing fear of tax avoidance. The legislator does not feel able to foresee the consequences of the complete abolition of joint taxation for unearned income and fears that tax avoidance could be facilitated. Another factor is that the introduction of complete separate taxation is not deemed necessary from a labour market point of view.

Denmark

In 1970 the married wife was acknowledged as a separate tax subject as regards income from independent trade and business and personal wages and salaries, pensions and similar personal income. At the same time it was acknowledged that 'the assisting housewife' working together with her husband could claim part of 'his' income as her separate income within a certain maximum. A joint taxation with the husband as tax subject is, however, still the fundamental rule in respect of income from capital and there are no provisions as for instance 'splitting' or similar reductions of the progressive tax in this area.

Finland

Spouses were taxed jointly until 1975 according to the rules of the national income and wealth taxes. The increased effect of the tax system's progressivity was, however, softened through the use of special tax scales and deductions for jointly taxed spouses. The principles of joint taxation, the complexity of the tax system and the fact that the scales and the deductions were not adequately adjusted to keep up with rising nominal income led, however, to increasingly intense criticism of these rules. This criticism and the desire to maintain the high labor participation rate of women resulted in the adoption of an income-splitting system in 1975, and, beginning in 1976, individual taxation of spouses' earned income was introduced. Unearned income in excess of 2000 mks (app. 500 US dollars) per year continues, however, to be jointly taxed, and the wealth tax also operates on a joint basis. It should also be noted that under certain conditions the above rules apply also to unmarried persons who live in a relationship which 'resembles that of marriage'.

According to the proportional local income tax system, spouses are – and always have been – taxed individually for all types of income.

Norway

In 1959 it became possible to choose to have individual taxation of the earned income of the spouse having the lowest earned income. Earned income here includes compensation for services, business income and the like. Wealth and unearned income, however, continue to be taxed on a joint basis, and no changes are expected in this area. Originally there was no possibility to have individual taxation of income from joint business activities, but in 1969 a limited option was made available, and this was liberalized somewhat in 1976. Income from the joint business activities of spouses is, however, not yet treated in the same way as is income from other sources. This creates problems from a control standpoint.

For several years prior to the 1959 revision womens' organisations had protested against mandatory joint taxation for reasons of principle, and it is clear that an important factor in the revision was the fact that increasingly large numbers of married women were taking jobs outside the home. It seems, however, that practical rather than theoretical arguments were the direct motivation for the change, for as late as 1954 a broadly representative commission had concluded that joint taxation was the most just solution.

Sweden

The emancipation of women is one of the most dominant features in Swedish social life during the last decades. Women are now gainfully employed to an extent unknown previously in Swedish history. Most Swedish families have nowadays two bread-winners, which is one of the most important explanations of the relatively high standard of living.

The old system of joint taxation was therefore heavily criticised from the standpoint of sexual equality. In 1970 the old system was abolished and separate taxation (in Sweden called 'individual taxation') was made mandatory. Separate taxation of spouses extends, however, only to earned income. Unearned income is still taxed jointly. The reason given for this remaining joint taxation is mainly the risk of tax avoidance.

The 1970 legislation did not extend individual taxation to business and farm income where one of the spouses was employed by the other, the deduction of a salary paid to the other spouse not being allowed. In 1976, however, individual taxation was introduced in that case also. If one of the spouses has been working at least 400 hours per year in the business or farm of the other spouse the business or farm income may be shared between the spouses. The helping spouse can be attributed income up to a maximum of the market value of the work performed.

The remaining elements of joint taxation (unearned income and net wealth) have been heavily attacked from the standpoint of sexual equality. A government committee recently considered itself unable, however, to propose its complete abolition as long as the tax avoidance problem has not been solved.

5. Taxation of Owner-Occupied Dwellings

It may be difficult for the non-Scandinavian reader to understand the great interest in and hot feelings about the taxation of owner-occupied dwellings in Denmark, Norway and Sweden. The effects of these rules are, however, extremely important as they give rise to important effects on the distribution of income and wealth.

The rules are in principle the same in all the Scandinavian countries. With the exception of Finland all interest is deductible. A certain imputed value of the use of the house is taxed as income. This imputed value is calculated as a certain percentage of the assessed value of the house. The result of these rules is that the deduction of the interest of the loans on the house from the imputed value of the use of the house often gives rise to large deficits. These deficits can be deducted from other income of the taxpayer. It should be borne in mind that the marginal tax rate of physical persons in the higher brackets of income is very high. The result is that persons living in homes of their own receive a very important tax advantage in comparison with those living in rented apartments.

This effect is most clearly seen in new houses, and it is supposed that the tax provisions have contributed to important increases in housing prices.

The increased prices for private homes give rise to new tax problems. For a variety of reasons such capital gains are generally not taxed. The result is that an important number of persons increase their net wealth considerably. This is an important factor in countries where the possibilities to accumulate wealth are rather limited due to the high marginal taxes on income. It might be added that the rise in housing prices gives benefits to the owners even before the house is sold. It is often possible to use the house as a first-class security for new loans which can be used to buy cars, sail boats and other costly items. Interest on the loans will be deductible and due to the high marginal tax rates the real cost of ownership will be very small.

It is true that these problems are not specific to owner-occupied dwellings. They are the same in all cases where property is bought with borrowed money. The cause of the problems is inflation or rather the lack of adaptability of the tax systems to inflation. When inflation was low or non-existent the rules were fair enough. The imputed income corresponded roughly to the general level of interest. No deficit arose and thus no tax advantage. There were no sharp rises in the price level of real property caused by inflation (though of course houses close to the big cities were attractive) and thus no tax-caused capital gains.

An important factor in the present situation is the treatment of indexed loans, which is generally very disadvantageous for the lender. The present conditions give rise to tax advantages for all indebted persons who have used their loans for investment in real values. On the other hand savers, especially holders of bank deposits, are losers.

It is an open question if the present problems will be solved. The enormous redistribution of wealth from savers to indebted investors might make important groups uninterested in finding a solution.

Denmark

It has already been mentioned above, that the capital gains on private houses till now have been excepted from ordinary and special income tax. Most private homes are heavily mortgaged and the interest level has been steadily climbing. This has led to results which have caused perhaps the most serious conflict in our age. Private interests are fully deductable and the imputed value of the use of the house is calculated in a way (by percentages of estimated tax value) which in many cases is far lower than the market level of rented apartments. This way the possession of a house produces a net loss which is set off against other income. The tax factor together with many other factors – for instance rapid growth of production costs – has sent the house prices skyrocketing.

It has been discussed slowly to abolish the right to deduct private interest but difficulty in distinguishing between private and business interests has till now been a barrier. An attempt to increase the imputed rent value of the owner-occupied dwellings has met determined political opposition. The problem has, however, grown to such proportions that it is no longer possible to neglect it.

Finland

The main principle, that imputed income is not included in the income tax base, generally applies also to imputed rent from owner-occupied residences. There are, however, several exceptions, though they are not particularly important from a practical standpoint. For example, the imputed income of a permanent residence is taxable to the owner-occupant only where the taxable value of the residence exceeds a specified 'luxury level'. Less than 3 % of all permanent dwellings may be expected to have a taxable value which exceeds this level. As regards other types of residences, e.g. summer homes, which are at the disposition of the taxpayer, income is fully taxable to him under the local tax system, and under the national tax system such income is taxed to the extent it exceeds a fixed sum. The taxable imputed income amount is equal to 3 % of the taxable value of the residence to the extent it exceeds this minimum amount.

In addition to the rules providing for the non-taxability of capital gains on the sale of homes and the relatively extensive deduction for interest on housing loans, investments in one's personal residence are favored by the tax system's rules concerning the wealth tax. These generally establish a taxable value on residences, and especially on permanent residences, which is substantially less than the market value of the property.

Norway

With regard to the imputed income of personal residences it was established as early as the 1920's that in practice the net income would be fixed at a certain percentage (usually 2½ – 3%) of the taxable value of the property, i.e. usually the value established for purposes of wealth taxation. This assumes, of course, that the property is used by the owner as his personal residence. Since the percentage rate applied was rather low compared with the actual rental value of the property and the taxation value did not keep pace in the long run with increases in the market value of the property, this practice led gradually to a significant undertaxation of this type of income. A committee proposal therefore suggested in 1973 that the percentage rate should be increased significantly, especially with respect to highly-valued properties, and that the taxation value should be increased to 80% of the market value.

This proposal led, however, to a storm of protests, and thus the result was that the existing practice was more clearly regulated by statute and was, in fact, somewhat liberalized. The problem of establishing the taxation value was made the subject of further study, and this study continues. In the interim the taxation value rules have not been substantially changed, thus giving rise to even further disparities in this area.

With respect to the taxation of gains on the sale of residential property one may refer to what was said in section 2 above. Thus, according to current law, gains on such a sale are nontaxable, provided it is used as the taxpayer's personal residence and he has held it for more than 10 years on the date of sale. If the taxpayer's personal residence is sold after a shorter holding period, the gains are taxable (for sales with a holding period of between 5 and 10 years only a portion of the gain is taxable), but taxation can be deferred for an indefinite period if the amount received is reinvested in a new personal residence. This latter rule was introduced into the law in 1966, and can easily lead to a situation where such gains are never taxed. This occurs, namely, where the reinvestment property is owned for more than ten years prior to being sold and is used as the taxpayer's personal residence for at least five of these years. Gains on the sale of rented residential property are, as mentioned above, always taxable, regardless of holding period, and there is no provision for deferral of taxation where the amount received is reinvested.

It should be mentioned in this connection that interest is deductible no matter how a loan is used. The result can easily be that the interest deductions on a mortgage or residential loan can exceed the taxable imputed income. This is primarily because the imputation of income on a personal residence is too low. For this reason as well as others there is from time to time discussion of establishing a 'ceiling' on deductible interest on such loans. At present (December 1978) a group within the Finance Department is working with this issue.

It cannot be denied that the favourable tax treatment of personal residences has been in part responsible for the significant price increases on the residential property market in recent years.

Sweden

The deficiencies of the Swedish tax system with regard to the treatment of inflation has given rise to serious problems, especially a completely unintended redistribution of wealth from savers to borrowers.

About half the Swedish population lives in houses of their own. A person living in his own house is taxed on an imputed income calculated by applying a certain percentage to the assessed value of the house. On the other hand all interest paid is deductible. When introduced these rules were fairly balanced. Interest rates increased, however, while the imputed income increased only for some categories of house-owners. The inflation of recent years has resulted in an important increase in interest rates. As interests are deductible, the result has been that especially newly-built one-family houses show big deficits which are deductible from other income of the tax-year.

The most important factor is, however, capital gain taxation. As already mentioned the acquisition cost of real property is multiplied by an index number to take account of inflation. The loans of the house-owner are not indexed, however. The result is that the house-owner in a rather short time makes an untaxed gain on the reduction in the real value of the loan.

On the other hand savers are taxed on an income that is not adjusted for inflation. They are taxed, for exemple, on the whole amount of interest received, notwithstanding the fact that the main part of this interest is really only a compensation for inflation.

6. Use of Taxation as an Economic Tool

As already stated the tax revenue produced by corporation taxation is rather insignificant in all the Scandinavian countries. On the other hand the economic impact of corporate decisions is great. This could be said to be the general background to the introduction of different tax measures with the aim of stimulating corporations to take certain decisions with the help of tax concessions.

Generally speaking two different types of tax measures can be distinguished. Economic stimulus is sometimes given by new tax laws, which are especially enacted with the purpose of giving stimulus for a limited period of time. Apart from such provisional legislation there exists also a permanent legislation with the purpose of giving corporations tax advantages if they make certain decisions in line with government economic policy. The system of investment reserves is the most well-known example of the latter kind of legislation.

In the beginning tax legislation was used primarily to stimulate investment during recessions and discourage investment during booms. Private investment was supposed to be a key factor in a business cycle. After some time, however, the general interest was focused on new types of problems, especially regional policy. The Scandinavian countries – at least Sweden, Finland and Norway – resemble each other in having vast underpopulated areas. In such areas the population has traditionally made their living in primary economic activities, farming, forestry and fishing. As the economic importance of these activities has rapidly decreased, a large part of the population in the sparsely populated areas has been forced to search for new employment opportunities in the big towns. As this development has been considered undesirable for many reasons, different measures have been used to provide new jobs in the underpopulated areas. Tax measures have, especially in the beginning, been used to a large extent. After some time, however, other methods have been employed, and the tax measures have become comparatively less important.

It can be said that the general familiarity with the tax legislation and the existence of a well-extablished administration makes it natural to use tax measures when a new public policy is introduced. As other and perhaps more sophisticated methods are worked out the tax measures are used to a lesser extent.

SPECIAL FEATURES OF THE SCANDINAVIAN DEVELOPMENT

Denmark

Tax legislation has in several ways been used as an investment stimulating tool. Accelerated depreciations and capital allowances are typical ways of stimulating production. In the years 1975 and 1976 ordinary depreciation (30% on declining balance) was increased 50%. And moreover, a deduction of 20% of the purchase price of new machinery was temporarily introduced without affecting the basis of depreciation. The general legislation permitting deduction of reservation of investment funds has been extended to 25% of net profit plus such expenses as interests. These funds can be made by depositing in a bank only 50% of the total reservation and they can be used without immediate-income effect by only lowering the basis of depreciation of the asset acquired for the capital placed in the investment fund. The Danish system functions, however, 'automatically' and is not as the Swedish directly influenced by government policy in respect of investments.

Finland

Since World War II the tax system has been used for purposes of economic regulation, especially in the areas of economic stabilization and regional and business policy. The tax legislation in the area of economic stabilization has two main components. The first consists of a number of laws giving the government the right to impose extra taxes and require mandatory stabilization deposits – on, for example, export income and investments in building construction – whenever the economy is considered overheated. The second includes the legislation – revised as of the beginning of 1978 – providing for nonmandatory investment funds. The current rules concerning investment funds are quite similar to the corresponding Swedish rules. The tax legislation in the regional policy area provides certain advantages to busineses which locate in the northern and eastern sections of the country, including, among others, favorable depreciation rules, certain extra investment deductions as well as certain wealth tax relief measures. Finally, in the area of business policy there is special tax legislation for, among others, the shipbuilding, metal and construction industries.

With regard to the taxation of individuals the nontaxability of interest on normal bank deposits and on bonds has already been mentioned. Other provisions which are at least in part aimed at affecting the behavior of individuals include excise taxes on alcohol, tobacco, margarine and gasoline, as well as the automobile and motorcycle tax.

Tax measures have also been used to dampen inflation. For example, the sales tax (turnover tax) on certain necessities, such as certain basic food stuffs and fuels, has been mitigated or abolished.

In recent years a significant policy has been carried out in order to stimulate the growth of the economy by using certain tax measures as means. The provisions have covered, for instance, decrease of sales tax on investment goods, decrease of social security contributions paid by employers, unlimited depreciation allowances for manufacturing, new possibilities for reserve creation in business taxation, increase of the deductions connected with corporate dividends, etc. Some of these measures are temporary, some others permanent changes.

In order to stimulate the growth of the disposable income of households a new type of policy is carried out since 1974 in connection with the personal income taxation. Besides the tax reforms mentioned above, one has tried to dampen the effect of inflation on the tax burden of households. The purpose of this is especially to dampen the effect of inflation on the tax burden of households. In Finland an indexation of the tax scales and deductions is not in force, but in each year the amount of tax reductions have been determined considered by taking into account the rate of inflation. The means by which this policy has been realized are the widening of the brackets in the tax scale, on one hand, and the increase of the main deductions and tax credits on the other.

Norway

A general system of tax advantages for saving a portion of income in 'investment funds' (usually up to 25% of income) was introduced in 1962. The objective was to utilize the tax system for economic stabilization purposes by releasing funds during recession periods. During recent years this general system has been suspended, with the exception of savings which are to be used for environmental purposes. Thus the effects of the system have been significantly changed.

In 1969 a law was passed which provided varying tax advantages for investments in various districts. Most important is the system of savings funds, but the law also provides tax advantages of other types, e.g. favourable depreciation rules.

In 1977 a system of investment deductions on the purchase of ships was introduced on a temporary basis in order to stimulate the shipbuilding industry, which was having difficulties. This system allowed a deduction of up to 25% of the purchase price of ships without effecting depreciation deductions, provided the responsible government department gave its approval. This system led to some purchases which otherwise would not have been made, but on the other hand it had the unexpected effect of producing a large number of taxpayers who owed no taxes.

In order to stimulate savings a system was introduced in 1967 providing deductions for amounts placed in bank accounts according to a savings agreement requiring that the funds should be held by the bank for at least ten years. The amount of this deduction was limited. A similar deduction had been available earlier for life insurance premiums, and it was also somewhat expanded. This system had always been controversial, and in 1974 it was changed to provide a tax credit of 40% of the amount placed in savings rather than an income deduction for the entire amount. Returns on personal savings have for a long time been partially exempted from taxation.

Recently a certain amount of skepticism seems to have developed toward using tax rules for purposes of regulation. This is due in part to doubt that such usage of tax rules is sufficiently effective and in part to the fact that it often brings with it undesirable side-effects.

Sweden

Tax methods have been widely used in Sweden to stimulate investment in times of recession. The Swedish system of investment reserves is fairly well-know internationally. This system gives a Swedish corporation the right to deduct allocations to investment reserves up to 40% of its profits. 46% of the amount deducted must be deposited to the account of the corporation with the Swedish central bank. The amount that has to be deposited is less than the tax that would otherwise been paid (about 58%) but bears no interest.

When the Government thinks it necessary from an economic point of view it can give the corporations permission to use their investment reserve. This means that the amount deposited with the Central Bank is paid out and that the investment reserve is used to depreciate the assets acquired by the corporation. This means that these assets are not depreciated according to the normal rules. Double deduction is thus avoided. As an extra stimulus an extra deduction of 10% of the used investment reserve is deductable from taxable income without any corresponding depreciation of assets.

The investment reserves have been used in different ways at different times. Originally they were mostly used to stimulate general investment activity in times of depression. In later years more emphasis has been put on the need to stimulate investment in certain disadvantaged regions.

Apart from the system of investment reserves investment has been stimulated by extra deductions according to special legislation passed from time to time. On the other hand in boom times some kinds of investment have been discouraged by special taxes.

7. Intensified Action against Tax Avoidance and Tax Evasion

All Scandinavian countries are high tax countries. An important feature is the high marginal tax rates for physical persons, especially in the higher income brackets. An important development in the Scandinavian countries is the growing importance of different measures aimed at making sure that all the taxes are really paid.

All the Scandinavian states employ the PAYE-system, i.e. the employer withholds tax when paying the employee his remuneration. This tax is only preliminary. If the assessment of the taxpayer based on his tax return shows that the final tax is bigger than the preliminary tax, additional tax has to be paid. Withholding taxes are not employed, however, for interests and dividends to residents. The PAYE system is an important factor ensuring the effectiveness of tax collection.

Tax audits by the personnel of the tax administration has been increasing. Information is also given to the tax authorities by third parties, i.e. banks and insurance companies, which are requested by law to supply information about the taxpayer.

The penal system has been used to a growing extent to make the taxpayers supply the necessary information for a correct assessment. As the courts would have been overburdened by all the cases, a system of administrative sanctions has been introduced in most Scandinavian countries.

If there are significant similarities between the Scandinavian countries in the methods of fighting tax evasion, this is not the case for fighting tax avoidance. In fact every Scandinavian country has employed different methods. Finland has gone furthest and has introduced á general clause against tax avoidance. It should be added, however, that owing to the fairly restrictive interpretation traditionally used by the Supreme Administrative Court the general clause is not often found to be applicable. The other Scandinavian courts do not have general clauses against tax avoidance. Norway and Denmark, however, have different traditions of interpretation than Finland and Sweden. As these countries employ more realistic methods of interpretation, the need for a general clause if not felt to the same extent as in Finland. In Sweden on the other hand which employs the same restrictive and formal methods of interpretation as in Finland there exists no general clause against tax avoidance. The legislator has been very active in fighting tax avoidance and filling loop-holes in the tax law system when loop-holes are found. It has been discussed, however, whether legislative action is enough. A general clause has been suggested in Sweden too. The question has, however, not yet been decided.

The trend is evident. More and more actions are taken against tax avoidance and tax evasion. There is no knowledge about the extent of such practices but there is a general feeling that they are increasing. This has, however, not been proved. This feeling as such represents a certain danger as it might loosen tax morals generally.

Denmark

There has been no general legislative action in Denmark or any proposal with the aim of preventing tax avoidance. Our court practice shows a strong tendency to interpret tax laws in a very realistic way so that the scope of the rules are not undermined by 'tax gimmicks'.

In respect of tax evasion the legislation has been strengthened again and again especially by far-reaching rules enabling the tax autorities to obtain information not only from the taxpayer but also from banks and other institutions. This together with a collection of tax at the source has definitely restricted the possibilities of evasion. Even so income from 'black labour' is undoubtedly a factor of considerable importance although it has not been acknowledged politically. A proposal to collect tax on interests at the source was not carried through, but an intensified control by compulsory information from all money institutions has apparently proved to be effective.

In the later years the major companies have been subject to very close tax revisions. The results have not till now indicated major attemps at tax evasion. Most cases have their background in accounting principles not acceptable when computing taxable income.

Finland

In contrast to the other Scandinavian countries Finland's income and sales tax legislation have long contained a general clause for the prevention of tax avoidance. According to this clause, the tax authorities are entitled to disregard – in addition to sham transactions – transactions which the taxpayer has entered into for the obvious purpose of avoiding taxes. Experience with this general clause has been predominantly positive. In addition to having had a certain preventive effect, it has made it possible to deal with at least the most flagrant forms of tax avoidance without complicated special legislation. The relatively small amount of criticism of the general clause is probably to be attributed to the fact that it has been applied with great caution.

With respect to international tax avoidance one can mention that the domestic legislation was changed in 1975 so that escape from taxation by means of emigration has to some extent been made more difficult. In the area of company taxation proposed rules have recently been published which would make it possible for tax authorities to more effectively control and attack concealed transfers of income to foreign countries. These proposed rules also provide that the Finnish power to tax be increased to include portfolio income to Finnish-owned base companies in tax haven countries.

In order to reduce income tax evasion, withholding tax procedures have been made more effective in recent years. At the same time tax auditing, especially of companies, has been intensified and the administrative and criminal penalty system has been sharpened. The Scandinavian cooperation treaty has played a role in combating international tax evasion, as have the relatively strict Finnish currency regulations.

Norway

A withholding tax system for individual taxpayers was introduced as of 1957. In recent years this prepayment obligation has been broadened to cover payments made in kind and certain obligations have been established to make prepayments on reimbursements. Moreover the duty to give information on reimbursements has been expanded. The same applies with respect to providing information on the income of spouses and children in the taxpayer's business and providing information concerning certain foreign contractors and their employees. In December, 1978 the government presented a proposal for a new law concerning tax administration. This proposal goes a step further in the direction of increased obligations to supply information, and it contains more modern rules on penalties and penalty taxes.

The courts have had a number of cases involving tax avoidance in recent years. In general it can be said that the courts have not restricted themselves to a strict literal interpretation of the legal provisions, but have placed significant weight on the actual circumstances. Thus they have not tried to avoid a flexible construction of the tax laws where this has been necessary to have a coherent system. This position on the part of the courts has unquestionably contributed to limiting attemps at tax avoidance.

Sweden

In Sweden the income taxation of physical persons is very high. In order to secure payment of the taxes Sweden employs a PAYE-system according to which an employer has to deduct a 'preliminary tax' before paying the salary to the employee. The system does not apply to capital income. There is no withholding tax on interest and the withholding tax on dividends applies only to non-residents.

In order to enforce tax payment a system of administrative sanctions have been introduced in 1971 for minor tax offences. Tax fraud is regarded as a crime and is handled in the same way as other crimes. When a tax crime is suspected the authorities have rather far-reaching possibilities to produce evidence.

The Swedish tax courts traditionally interpret and apply tax laws in a formal and restrictive way. From time to time new ingenious methods of tax avoidance are discovered. In such cases the courts generally do not find that they have the possibility to stop the avoidance measures. It is supposed to be the task of the tax legislator to fill the loop-holes in the tax laws, not the task of the courts. The legislator generally acts very rapidly in such a case.

The growing amount of special tax legislation directed against different forms of tax avoidance has, however, increased the volume of the tax laws and made them even more difficult to understand. It has therefore been proposed to change the present Swedish way of combatting tax avoidance and introduce a special law against tax avoidance. There has been, however, much discussion of the advantages and disadvantages of such a law. The government has rewritten the first draft proposed by an expert committee, and the second draft is now being discussed. For the present no one knows if a special law against tax avoidance will be introduced or not.

In the international field there are some special provisions against tax avoidance. Prices that are not 'at arm's length' can be attacked, and Swedish-controlled foreign holding companies in some very special cases may be taxed in Sweden. In the international field the most important factors are the exchange controls which hinder tax-related capital movements.

8. International Co-operation

The Scandinavian countries have shown great interest in international co-operation in the tax field. The number of tax treaties has increased substantially, especially in recent years. The treaties generally follow the OECD model treaty.

Sweden and Finland seem to follow similar paths. Both countries have switched to the credit of tax method from the exemption method and have accepted a tax sparing credit in their treaties with developing countries. In their internal legislation they have as Denmark introduced methods to prevent advantages of tax emigration to a certain extent.

Co-operation between the Scandinavian states has been particularly important. The Scandinavian multilateral treaty on administrative assistance could be regarded as an important step forward. Much effort has been made to work out a multilateral treaty on income and capital based on the OECD draft convention. This treaty is in its final stage of preparation.

Denmark

Domicile is the leading criteria for tax liability. An emigrant may, however, be taxable during four years after emigration, unless he proves that he has become liable to income tax in another country. These provisions have not caused any changes in the treaties.

A general unilateral credit for income taxes was introduced in 1960. The right to deduct foreign (and national) taxes from income was abolished in 1967.

As of March, 1979 Denmark had concluded 37 general treaties and 5 treaties on estates and inheritances and a great number of special treaties. The majority are based on the OECD models. There seems to exist a tendency to adopt the credit method in treaties from the later years. Denmark has concluded a treaty with the Faroe Islands although they are part of the Danish Kingdom and a treaty with Greenland is under preparation. Treaties have been concluded with several East bloc countries (Hungary, Poland and Rumania) and several new treaties are under negotiation (Bulgaria, Czekoslovakia, Marocco, Tunisia). A new revised treaty with USA is under preparation.

Denmark is the only Scandinavian member of EC. The directives on capital transfer duty, general VAT (also on services) and on mutual assistance and tax avoidance have been adopted in national tax legislation. Several other directives under preparation may soon influence the tax law for example on corporate mergers and mother and daughter companies, taxation in border areas, and perhaps most important a uniform tax basis in respect of business income.

Tax problems in connection with multinational enterprises have been in the foreground and several investigations are being made on the EC and the OECD level. Danish central assessment authorities started in 1978 'arm's length' cases against four of the major oil companies making assessments by using an arbitrary gross profit method. It is generally regarded as very doubtful if these assessments will be confirmed by the tax court and even so these cases will no doubt be appealed to the Supreme Court if the assessments are sustained.

Finland

At present Finland has tax treaties covering income and wealth taxation with the following countries: Austria, Belgium, Brasil, Canada, Czeckoslovakia, Denmark, Egypt, France. Iceland, India, Ireland, Israel, Italy, Japan, Malta, the Netherlands, Norway, Poland, Portugal, Rumania, the Soviet Union, Spain, Sweden, Switzerland, Tanzania, the United Kingdom, the United States and West Germany.

During the past decade Finland has attempted to conclude tax treaties which to the greatest possible extent conform to the OECD's model tax convention. Except for certain reservations required because of Finland's special housing companies, Finland has stated a reservation against the OECD's model convention of 1977 only as to art. 9 (2) (associated enterprises) and art. 12 (royalties). These reservations are based primarily on control considerations rather than differing views on issues of principle.

In recent years Finland has gone over to application of the tax credit method, and in treaties with less developed countries Finland has generally accepted the inclusion of provisions concerning the tax sparing credit.

Norway

Norway has concluded some thirty bilateral tax treaties. Most of these have been concluded during the past 15 years, only seven are from the period prior to 1963. The great majority of Norway's tax treaties are based on the OECD's model tax convention. In the treaties with developing countries, however, there have been various deviations from this model convention in the direction of greater withholding tax possibilities. A new aspect of the situation is that Norway has recently signed a tax treaty with an East European country, namely, Poland.

The Norwegian tax treaties practically always operate according to tne exemption method on the Norwegian side.

It can be generally said that oil activities have been a significant factor in the increasing importance of international tax issues in Norway.

Sweden

In the year 1966 important changes were made in the principles of Swedish international taxation. In internal tax law the credit of taxsystem was introduced. The right, previously established, to deduct foreign taxes from Swedish taxable income, was not abolished, however, but kept as an alternative measure to mitigate international double taxation.

At the same time two important rules were introduced, the so-called three-year rule and the so-called one-year rule. The three-year rule is a rule of presumption. The first three years after leaving Sweden a Swedish citizen is supposed to remain a Swedish resident and thus subject to unlimited tax liability in Sweden. The presumption is rebuttable if the Swedish citizen can prove that he has severed his ties with Sweden.

The one-year rule exempts from tax liability in Sweden income earned abroad paid by a private employer provided that a person has stayed abroad for more than one year and been employed abroad for more than one year. In such a case the tax-payer is regarded as a Swedish resident.

Sweden has a great number of tax treaties. They are more than 40 and Sweden is in this respect one of the leading countries of the world. Generally speaking Sweden has tried to follow the OECD model treaty. In some cases, however, Sweden has deviated from the model. In treaties with developing countries the tax sparing credit has been acknowledged and the source countries have been given greater rights to tax. In the treaties with socialist countries the concept of permanent establishment has not been used to the same extent as in the model treaty. Other deviations from the model treaty are caused by the Swedish wish to enforce some of its principles of internal law. Most important in this respect is the Swedish desire to tax emigrated Swedish citizens according to the three-year rule and to tax pensions paid from Sweden. These principles are supposed to be so important from a Swedish point of view that Sweden did dot hesitate to renounce the treaty with Spain in 1965 prefering non-treaty conditions to an unsatisfactory treaty. A new treaty with Spain has, however, now been signed.